12/2013
B
03/2011

How Two-Feather was saved from loneliness

© 1990 C.J. Taylor

Published in Canada by Tundra
Books, Montreal, Quebec H3G 1R4

Published in the United States by
Tundra Books of Northern New York,
Plattsburgh, N.Y. 12901

Distributed in the United Kingdom by
Ragged Bears Ltd., Andover,
Hampshire SP11 9HX

Distributed in France by Le
Colporteur Diffusion, 84100 Orange

ISBN 0-88776-254-9
Library of Congress Catalog Number:
90-70138

Also available in a French edition,
Deux Plumes et la solitude disparue
ISBN 0-88776-255-7

**Canadian Cataloging in
Publication Data:**

Taylor, C.J., 1952-
 How Two-Feather was saved
from loneliness
ISBN 0-88776-254-9

 I. Title.

PS8589.A8817H69 1990
C90-090158-6   PZ7.T39Ho 1990
√j398'.26'089973

The publisher has applied funds from
its Canada Council block grant for
1990 toward the editing and
production of this book.

Design by Michael Dias

Printed in Hong Kong by South China
Printing Co. (1988) Ltd.

In memory of Michelle

How Two-Feather was saved from loneliness

An Abenaki Legend

C.J. Taylor

Tundra Books

Long ago the earth was a cold and lonely place. No one knew how to make fire. There were very few people and they wandered far in search of food.

Two-Feather was lonely and hungry. All winter long he had met no one. All he had to eat was the bark he cut off the trees and the roots he dug out from under the snow.

He was glad when at last spring came. The sun grew warmer and the ice melted from the lakes and rivers. As he knelt to drink from a rushing stream, he caught sight of his face in the water and he felt lonely again: "How I wish," he thought, "I could see another face."

To forget his loneliness, Two-Feather lay down to sleep on the soft moss. He was awakened by a voice calling his name. He was afraid to open his eyes and find it was only a dream. But the voice came again and the rustle of leaves told him someone was near.

He opened his eyes and was frightened to find a strange figure above him. His fear passed as he saw a woman, lovely as spring, with long soft hair. He held out his arms to her, but she moved away.

He tried again and again to touch her, but always she stayed just beyond his reach. All day he followed her.

At nightfall they came to a lake. He could not get close to her,

so he made a drum and, in the moonlight, sang of his love.

"Please," he begged. "I am so lonely and you are so lovely. Stay with me and I will love you and look after you forever."

"I have come to look after you, Two-Feather," she said softly. "If you do what I say, you will never be lonely again."

"What would you have me do?" he asked.

"Follow me," she said, and turned away.

He followed her over mountains, through forests, across streams, always afraid she would get away from him. If he tried to catch up with her, she hurried on ahead. But when he grew tired or hungry and slowed down to rest or eat, she waited for him. After many days, they came to a vast meadow.

At last she stopped and rose up into the air, hovering over him like a bird.

"Two-Feather," she said, "gather some dry grass into a little pile, then take two sticks and rub them together."

Soon sparks flew. The little pile of grass caught fire. Then the tall grass and soon the whole meadow was ablaze. Two-Feather had never seen fire before and he was frightened. Would it spread forever and destroy the earth?

But the soft voice reassured him. "It will be all right, Two-Feather," she said.

When all the grass in the meadow had burned and the fire died down, she spoke again.

"Now, take hold of my hair and pull me over the burned ground."

"I cannot do that," Two-Feather protested. "I cannot hurt you for I love you."

"If you love me, Two-Feather, you must trust me and do as I say," she said gently.

Two-Feather did as she asked. He pulled her back and forth over the burned meadow. Her hair in his hand was softer than anything he had ever felt before. She seemed to grow lighter and lighter as he pulled.

When he finished and turned, she was no longer there. But where he had pulled her, green shoots appeared. It was the first corn ever grown.

As the corn grew tall and ripened, people found their way to it. Now they no longer had to wander in search of food. They built houses and a village.

Two-Feather married and had children. He was no longer lonely but he never forgot the Corn Goddess. Each summer as he held the first ears of corn, he felt in his hands again the softness of her hair.

The Abenaki

What is unusual about this Abenaki tale
is that it combines three origins into one
legend and makes them inseparable: the
origin of fire, the origin of corn and the
origin of communal life. Plowing was not yet
known, and one of the few ways the Indians
could clear the land for planting was by
burning the vegetation. And only when
farming was possible could they switch from
the nomadic life of the hunter and gatherer
to settle into communities. The legend, one
of the loveliest in Indian folklore, is also a
tender story of love and longing.

The territory of the Abenaki stretched from
the coast of Maine west to Lake Champlain
in New York State, north to Quebec and
south to North Carolina. The Eastern
Abenaki tribes were "inhabitants of rivers
and smaller streams" and lived by hunting
and fishing until after the arrival of the
Europeans. However, some Western
Abenaki tribes raised considerable crops of
maize earlier. So the legend would appear to
have originated with them.

Sources of information: *Indians of Canada*
by Diamond Jenness; and "The Eastern
Abenaki" by Dean R. Snow and "The
Western Abenaki" by Gordon M. Day
from volume 15 of the *Handbook of
North American Indians* edited by
William C. Sturtevant.

How Two-Feather was saved from loneliness
is a retelling of the legend "The Origin of
Corn" from Brown, *Journal of American
Folklore,* volume 3, as reprinted in *Tales of
the North American Indians,* compiled by
Stith Thompson.